Luna

The Mare with the Sky Blue Eyes
A True Story

Story by Dora Dillistone

~

Paintings by Jonathan Warm Day Coming

Copyright © 2019 by Dora Dillistone
All rights reserved.
This book or any portion thereof may not be reproduced or used in any manner whatsoever without the express written permission of the publisher except for the use of brief quotations in a book review.

Printed in Korea
First Printing, 2019

ISBN 978-0-578-58088-3

Author: Dora Dillistone
Illustrations: Jonathan Warm Day Coming

Layout and design: Wiz Allred

Printed by Four Colour Group • Louisville, Kentucky

Published by
Desert Moon Graphics
310 Leatherman St.
Taos, NM 87571

The shy little mare with the piercing blue eyes
stood shining like silver in the high desert sun.
She was hungry and thin when The Horse Shelter had taken her in.

The humans were kind and loving so her thoughts were filled with hope.
Her stomach was filled with hay.

Maybe someday she would have a real home.

One spring day, the trainers came to visit The Horse Shelter near Santa Fe,
carefully looking for the special horse
to show off their training skills.

She was too small, too thin and too quiet.
No one looked at her.
They just walked by.

Suddenly a too-tall young trainer glanced into her blue eyes.

She looked at him and thought,

"Please, sir, pick me and I will try very hard."

"I am small but I will carry you well."

The too-tall young trainer spoke to her

and in a whisper he said,

"There is something special about you, little mare."

"Come with me and I will teach you my secrets."

"We will train together and find you a good home.

But, we only have three months to try."

It was a warm summer day in June when they drove north to Taos, the trainer, his wife, two boys and the little white mare. MorningStar Stables was to be their new home where the family would live and the horses would train.

The show and the auction that might give her a home were less than three months away.

More horses arrived daily to the MorningStar Stables
to learn of the trainer's secrets.

Close by the barn stood a strange lady.
Her curious husband was right by her side.
They welcomed the new arrivals and gave them a hand
as the horses unloaded and found their new stalls.

The stable was small but filled with love for all of the horses.
The little mare thought:
"It is a good place to stay
even if only for a few months."

The too-tall young trainer had started her lessons with a lead rope and halter.
Circles she did in a round pen for him.
She walked then trotted and finally cantered
as everyone smiled and patted her head.

A saddle was gently placed on her back
and the too-tall young trainer carefully climbed on.
Into the arena they went!

She wobbled at first but grew very strong.
They worked every day
and she never complained.

There were challenges the trainer knew the mare must do.
Quickly she learned and never grew tired.

She stood on a tarp and looked at the mountains.
Her tiny hooves pranced across the wooden bridge
and over the pole she jumped.

Once, twice, three times she jumped!

Only two months were left before the horse show and auction.
She thought to herself,
"Could someone really want a little horse like me?"

The little mare made new friends at the stables.
Figaro the barn cat visited her everyday.
The chocolate-colored Rocky Mountain horse
named Jude became her best friend.
They would run, kick, and buck.
"Jude, look what I can do. You can do it too!"
Over the bridge they would run and around the arena they would fly.
Star, the big black horse would run beside them.
He, too, was her friend and wanted to play.

"Training is fun," said the too-tall young trainer
who taught her so well.
"She learns very fast and works really hard."

Jude taught her how to whinny.
"My what a deep voice you have" he said.
Star would watch over her as she slept in her pen.
"I am strong and will keep you safe as you sleep."

The little mare thought:
"Why should I ever have to leave?"

The mare grew and became more beautiful
–in an unusual sort of way.
No longer did her ribs show since she
ate her hay every day.
Her metallic coat was washed and groomed to a shining glow.

The strange lady watched and wondered:
"What is this little mare with the shining silver hair and the piercing blue eyes
who tries so hard to do her very best?"
"There's something special about her", said the curious husband.

"What can it be?"

Finally the day of The Horse Shelter show and auction came.
The pale little mare was bathed and groomed
and combed and sprayed.
"Today I will do my best," she thought to herself.

The too-tall young trainer's beautiful wife had given the mare a special song to dance to:
"Volare", which means to fly.

And that is just what the little mare with the sky blue eyes did.
She flew around the arena!
She circled and trotted then cantered to the music.
She side-passed and halted, then cantered some more.

The crowd cheered and applauded and stood on their feet.
"Bravo, Bravo!" they cheered!

After the show came time for the auction.
Funds would be raised for all
of the horses at the shelter
to feed them and make them healthy and safe.

The bidding began.

The little mare stood quietly.
Her piercing blue eyes looked at the crowd.
Would she go home with a new family?
Would she ever see the MorningStar Stables again?

The strange lady and her curious husband
stood waiting and watching.
The bidding was fast and many were eager to adopt the little mare.

Suddenly she heard a loud yell!

"Sold" said the auctioneer!

Walking towards her was the strange lady and her curious husband.
They shook the trainer's hand and gave her a little pat on the head.
Could it be true? Would she see Jude and Star again?
Would Figaro again visit her every day?

She thought of the other horses,
and the children running and calling to her.
The beautiful mountains of Taos behind the arena she longed to see.

The strange lady took her lead rope and said,
"Come little girl we are taking you home."

And back to the MorningStar Stables they went.

The lady, no longer strange, came to visit her every day.
The curious husband grew more curious
about the little shining mare with the piercing blue eyes
who would stand in her pen and gaze at the moon.

One night the lady watched the mare glowing in the light of the moon and said, "we will call you Luna."
"Why are you so unusual Luna?"
"What makes your hair glow and shine in the light?"

"I know," said the curious husband, "we will ask the University what you are."
It did not hurt when they pulled the mane hair to send to the genetics laboratory.
Everyone waited anxiously for the test results from the University to arrive.

Finally the results came.

"Luna", the lady said,
"you have the DNA of the oldest domestic horses."

"The Turkoman and the Arabian horses from lands far away and long, long ago gave you their genes."
"You carry the blood of the golden horses.
You have the heart, soul and bravery of horses that carried their warriors and lived by their tents.
They lived in the desert and looked up at mountains like those in the land where you now live.
Their beauty and bravery were known throughout the world."

Luna heard stories that were told to the children
of ancient horses in faraway lands and thousands of years ago.
Stories of the Silk Road and Arabian Nights
and songs of deserts and mountains
just like the ones where she now lives.

Luna's perlino-colored coat gives off a metallic shine
like the horses so admired by Alexander the Great.
He called these horses "the most beautiful" horses.
They were strong and courageous as they carried their warriors and conquered new lands.

The coming winter will not hurt Luna for she is a strong little mare.
She shares the strength of her ancestors before her.

Fall was approaching and Luna could hear the sounds
of San Geronimo Feast Day at the Taos Pueblo.
It was September and the leaves were turning gold.
Luna looked up at the moon in the clear cold mountain air.
Tonight, the snow-topped mountains will cast long shadows from the light of the moon.

Coyotes sang in the distance.
Deer grazed in the back pasture while the stables settled in for the night.

One night a young bear visited the horses while out searching for apples falling from trees.
Jude, Luna and Star watched over the barn but knew there was nothing to fear.
"Brother Bear," Jude spoke, "we know you are our friend and will do us no harm."
"I am just getting fat for my long winter sleep,"
said the cinnamon colored bear.

Winter snows came early to Taos but Luna grew a thick coat
of shining hair to keep her warm.

Other horses came to train and then went home.
She loved the MorningStar, all the horses and Figaro the cat.
She loved Taos Mountain, Lobo Peak and the snow capped Wheeler Peak.
Most of all she loved her humans.
Luna knew this was forever her home.

The full moon of the winter solstice had passed and it was Christmas Eve.
All was quiet.
The bonfires glowed in the distance at the Taos Pueblo and Luna could smell the aromatic wood of the fires.
The sound of the drums traveled through the thin crisp night air.
A shooting star sped across the dark night sky.

On Christmas day the lady and her curious husband gave Luna a beautiful new saddle made just to fit her.
Snow began to fall and Luna caught the flakes on her nose.

Tomorrow Luna would run and play in the thick new fallen snow.
Jude and Star would run with her.

The days were getting longer.
Spring was coming
to MorningStar Stables.

The land was wakening to new life.
Magpies revisited their nest to prepare it for their eggs.
Ravens plucked hair from the horses' tails to build waterproof nests.
Sounds of wild turkeys, baby goats, and lambs filled the air.
The pink blossoms of the apple and cherry trees opened against a crystal blue sky
and promised that this year there would be plenty of fruit for all.
Soon the hummingbirds would return.

Luna watched as new horses came to the stable to train.
The too-tall young trainer will choose another horse from The Horse Shelter near Santa Fe
for the show and auction this year.
But Luna knew she would not leave her family.

The little mare, no longer shy, gazes up at the mountain with her piercing blue eyes.
She is no longer thin and no longer hungry for she is very well fed
and very much loved
by all of her family with both four legs and two.

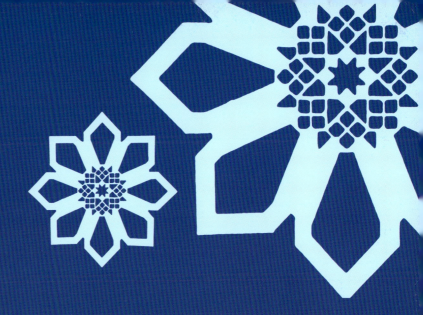

Today Luna and the lady will ride together to celebrate her first year at MorningStar Stables.

She holds her head high as did her ancestors of long ago.
The lady and Luna have much to learn, but their journey together has just begun.

In Tribute

Luna was adopted from The Horse Shelter following her performance at the 2018
"Gimme Shelter Trainer Challenge". She lives with her trainer, Rudy Lara Jr.
and his family Aubriana, Joaquin and Santiago and adoptive parents, Dora and Carl Dillistone.
The MorningStar Stables is located in Taos, New Mexico, a town with a rich
cultural and ethnic history.
Her training and story continues with her loving human and horse family.

This book is dedicated to The Horse Shelter, to all the volunteers and trainers
who work with the horses, and to the horses they have saved.

Special Thanks to :

Deb Munroe and her mighty horse Casey who started me on this journey.
Rudy Lara Jr. and his beautiful wife Aubriana with their two young sons, Joaquin and Santiago.
They brought Luna to my attention.
My husband Carl who supports my endeavors and his horse Jude, the comic of the family.
Dr. Bessie Babits, our vet, who tells me there is no question that is too "dumb"
and is always there when we need her.
Kendall Sill: I am forever grateful for showing what a love of horses can mean for a young girl
and strong young woman and for maintaining her desire to help all animals.
I thank you for all of the time we spent reading books.
My undying appreciation goes to Walker Lee who helped me with my first rescue horse, Star,
and with Light Hands Horsemanship.
He taught me patience. It is never too late and never give up.
My horse Star who taught me so much about horse and human relationships.
To my Mom and Dad who encouraged my strange and inquisitive behavior but could
never afford to give me a horse.
Acknowledgement to Texas A&M University animal genetics laboratory.

For everyone who loves horses, real and imaginary.

About the Author:
Dora Dillistone

Photo: Carl Dillistone

Author Dora Dillistone is an artist who relocated from Houston, Texas to Taos, New Mexico with her husband Carl in 2009. After being a working artist and studying art processes for over thirty-five years, this relocation demanded a dramatic change in life. Dora became an active participant in every aspect of art in Taos. Dora had a late life introduction to horses when she adopted an injured horse (Star) from the Equine Spirit Sanctuary in Taos. It was love at first sight and Dora became aware of the intricate relationship between horses and humans. When her husband purchased a Rocky Mountain horse (Jude), they both became immersed in learning to ride and in everything about horses. This brought about the purchase of MorningStar Stables. In 2018, a trainer (Rudy Lara Jr.) moved to the stables to train horses and brought with him a strange little mare (Luna). Dora's artwork continues and revolves around her environment including earth, wind, rain and fire. Luna's story is a true record of her adoption into the Dillistone family and an observation of events during her first year in Taos.

You can read about Dora's life and work at:
www.doradillistone.com

Editors: Nancy Allen, author • David Perez, author
Book Design: Wiz Allred • Desert Moon • Taos/Santa Fe

About the Artist:
Jonathan Warm Day Coming

Artist and writer Jonathan Warm Day Coming has been working from his home on Taos Pueblo most of his life. He is the father of two daughters, Carly and Nuna. In 1995 he was honored as being the inaugural Taos Talking Pictures Film Festival Poster Artist. He served on the Advisory Board and then on the Board of Directors of Taos Talking Pictures Film Festival.

Jonathan's art has been exhibited in museums across the country. A highlight was a history-making exhibition at the Harwood Museum of Art in Taos, New Mexico of his paintings along with those of his mother, Eva Mirabal (Eah-Ha-Wa), who passed away in 1968.

Jonathan has written and illustrated several children's books, and has also illustrated books by other writers. Currently he is collaborating with the esteemed author Lois Palken Rudnick on a book tentatively titled, *Eva Mirabal: Three Generations of Tradition and Modernity at the Taos Pueblo* to be published by the Museum of New Mexico Press.

See more of Jonathan's work at:
www.jonathanwarmday.com

Photo: Barbara Sparks